EDGE
BOOKS™

Top Hybrid Dogs

LABRADOODLE

Labrador Retrievers
Meet
Poodles!

by Sue Bradford Edwards

CAPSTONE PRESS
a capstone imprint

Edge Books are published by Capstone Press,
1710 Roe Crest Drive, North Mankato, Minnesota 56003
www.mycapstone.com

Library of Congress Cataloging-in-Publication Data
Names: Edwards, Sue Bradford, author.
Title: Labradoodle : labrador retrievers meet poodles! / by Sue Bradford
   Edwards.
Description: North Mankato, Minnesota : Edge Books, an imprint of Capstone
   Press, [2019] | Series: Top hybrid dogs | Includes bibliographical
   references and index. | Audience: Age 8-14. | Audience: Grade 7 to 8.
Identifiers: LCCN 2018036901 (print) | LCCN 2018037746 (ebook) | ISBN
   9781543555264 (ebook) | ISBN 9781543555196 (hardcover : alk. paper)
Subjects: LCSH: Labradoodle--Juvenile literature. | Designer dogs--Juvenile
   literature.
Classification: LCC SF429.L29 (ebook) | LCC SF429.L29 E39 2019 (print) | DDC
   636.72/8--dc23
LC record available at https://lccn.loc.gov/2018036901

Editorial Credits
Editor: Maddie Spalding
Designer and Production Specialist: Laura Polzin

Photo Credits
iStockphoto: Bigandt_Photography, 20–21, Darren Brown, cover, fotografixx,
22–23, Michelle Hovet, 28–29, monkeybusinessimages, 4–5, PierceHSmith, 16–17,
rbulthuis, 24–25, Steve Debenport, 26–27; Newscom: Atkison Helen/SIPA, 9,
LWA/Sharie Kennedy Blend Images, 11; Shutterstock Images: Bigandt.com, 18,
Hollysdogs, 14–15, Jeanne Provost, 12–13, KariDesign, 26, Saranellieart, 19, The Dog
Photographer, 6–7

Design Elements
bittbox

Printed in the United States of America.
PA48

TABLE OF CONTENTS

CHAPTER ONE

MEET THE LABRADOODLE

Do you like dogs with shaggy fur coats and floppy ears? Then the Labradoodle may be the perfect dog for you and your family. These dogs are affectionate and energetic companions. It's no wonder that Labradoodles are among the world's most popular dogs.

Labradoodles are a type of hybrid dog. A hybrid dog is a cross between two **breeds**. The breeds are usually chosen for certain traits, or qualities. A Labradoodle is a cross between a Labrador retriever and a poodle. Labradors and poodles are **purebred** dogs. Labradoodles get their traits from both breeds.

breed – a type of dog that has specific traits

purebred – a dog that is the same breed as its parents

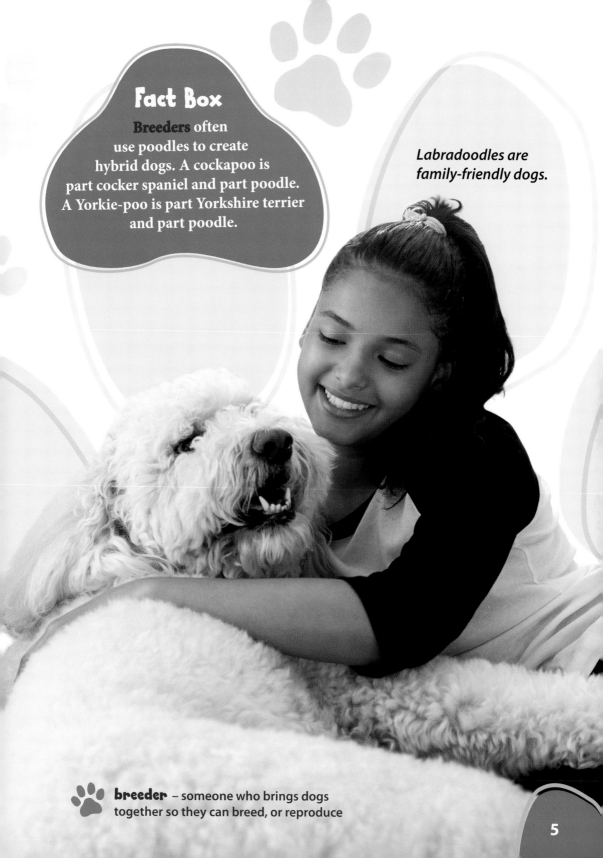

Labradoodles are family-friendly dogs.

breeder – someone who brings dogs together so they can breed, or reproduce

The Australian Labradoodle

In the United States, breeders sell Labradoodles that have poodle and Labrador retriever parents. These Labradoodle puppies can each have very different traits. For this reason, the U.S. Labradoodle is not a breed. To be a breed, the dogs each have to have the same traits. In Australia, people breed Labradoodles with other Labradoodles to try to create a Labradoodle breed.

Labradoodles tend to have thick and wavy fur.

WHY CHOOSE A LABRADOODLE?

People choose Labradoodles for many reasons. Some people who have dog allergies choose Labradoodles. People with dog allergies react to a dog's saliva and dander. Dander is tiny flakes of dry skin. People with dog allergies may react to dander after they pet a dog. Their skin may get itchy. They may get watery eyes. Some people may have trouble breathing. Poodles and some other breeds shed less fur than other types of dogs. Dogs that shed less fur produce less dander. Some Labradoodles get this trait from poodles. These dogs are less likely to bother someone who is allergic to dogs.

Purebred dogs can have certain health problems. Some people choose hybrid dogs because they believe these dogs are less likely to have such health problems. Whatever your reason for choosing the Labradoodle, there's a lot to love about this adorable dog.

CHAPTER TWO

LABRADOODLE HISTORY

In 1988 a woman named Pat Blum needed a **guide dog**. She had limited vision. Blum and her husband lived in Hawaii. Her husband was allergic to every breed of guide dog available in Hawaii. Blum had to search outside of Hawaii to find a guide dog. But she would have trouble bringing a dog from somewhere else into the state. No animal in Hawaii has ever had rabies. This virus can be deadly to dogs and humans. There are rules to keep the virus out of Hawaii. If a dog comes from someplace where rabies has been found, such as the rest of the United States, the dog must be put into **quarantine**. Blum did not want to put a dog through this.

guide dog – a dog that helps people with vision problems move around safely

quarantine – a place where an animal is kept alone until proven healthy so it doesn't spread disease

Some labradoodles are service dogs.

Blum learned that dogs from Australia can come into Hawaii without having to be quarantined. This is because the rabies virus hasn't spread to Australia. Blum contacted the Royal Guide Dog Association of Australia. This group bred and trained guide dogs. Blum hoped the association could help her find a guide dog that wouldn't trigger her husband's allergies.

BREEDING A NEW DOG

Wally Conron was the association's puppy breeding manager. People contacted him whenever they needed a guide dog. Conron went to work to find Blum a dog. He knew that a standard poodle would be big enough to serve as a guide dog. He also thought a poodle would be perfect because not many people are allergic to poodles. Conron took fur and saliva samples from 33 different standard poodles. He sent the samples to Mr. Blum's doctors. All of the samples triggered the man's allergies, so none of the poodles would work.

Labradoodles can make good pets for people with allergies.

Conron didn't give up. He knew that Labrador retrievers are smart and easily trained. So he decided to try crossing a Labrador retriever with a standard poodle. Three puppies were born. Conron again sent fur and saliva samples to Hawaii. Mr. Blum reacted to two of the puppies but not to the third. A possible guide dog had been found. Conron named this puppy Sultan.

Fact Box

Wally Conron bred 31 Labradoodle puppies in total. Today he has a Labrador retriever. He has never had his own pet Labradoodle.

A female Labradoodle usually gives birth to six to eight puppies at a time.

Sultan worked well for the Blums. Conron hoped this type of dog could help other people too. He bred another **litter**. Ten puppies were born. Only three were low allergy. Conron had hoped more of the dogs would be low allergy.

Sultan was soon in the news. People became excited about this new dog breed. The Labradoodle's intelligence and friendly personality made it popular. People started breeding Labradoodles in the United States. Today Labradoodles are bred as family-friendly pets. Some are also bred to be therapy dogs. Therapy dogs help comfort people who are sick or who have disabilities.

Fact Box

In 2009 a new game piece was created for the board game Monopoly. The piece was made to look like a Labradoodle.

 litter – a group of puppies born from the same mother

CHAPTER THREE

ALL ABOUT THE LABRADOODLE

Labradoodles are friendly dogs. They seem happy and excited when they are around people. It isn't just their owners they appear to adore. Many act open and friendly toward everyone they meet.

Labradoodles enjoy playing. But their high level of energy can sometimes be a problem. A playful Labradoodle can jump up on people when it gets excited. Luckily Labradoodles are often easy to train.

Labradoodles are smart and curious dogs.

Labradoodle Heroes

Labradoodles are known for their intelligence. This trait has helped them save people's lives. Two Labradoodles came to a stranger's rescue in January 2018. It was early morning in a small Michigan town. The dogs barked until they woke their owners, Lonnie and Susan Chester. One of the dogs tugged on Lonnie's sleeve until the man got out of bed. He followed the dogs to the door. The dogs ran outside when Lonnie opened the door. The dogs led Lonnie to a woman who was lying on the Chesters' driveway. Lonnie carried the woman inside. He knew she needed help. He called the police. It was 9 degrees Fahrenheit (−13 degrees Celsius) outside. Without the help of the two dogs, the woman could have died.

BIG AND SMALL

Labradoodles come in three different sizes. This is because their poodle parents can vary in size. Standard Labradoodles are usually 21 to 24 inches (53 to 61 centimeters) tall. Height is measured to the top of a dog's shoulder. The weight of a standard Labradoodle can vary from about 50 to 65 pounds (23 to 29 kilograms).

Medium Labradoodles are typically 17 to 20 inches (43 to 51 cm) tall. They often weigh between 30 and 45 pounds (14 and 20 kg).

Miniature Labradoodles are usually 14 to 16 inches (36 to 41 cm) tall. Their weight can vary from about 15 to 25 pounds (7 to 11 kg).

Labradoodles are small when they are puppies, but they get bigger quickly.

COATS AND COLORS

Labradoodles can also vary in coat color and **texture**. Some have soft and silky coats. Their fur is wavy or curly. This type of coat is called a fleece coat. Other Labradoodles have a coat that feels like a lamb's wool. This type of coat is called a wool coat. A Labradoodle with a wool coat will have curlier fur than a dog with a fleece coat.

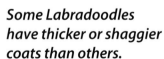

Some Labradoodles have thicker or shaggier coats than others.

 texture – the feel of something, such as a dog's fur

Another Labradoodle coat type is called the hair coat. Fur in a hair coat is straight or slightly wavy. A hair coat isn't as silky as a fleece coat. Labradoodles with a hair coat tend to shed a lot. They are the most likely of the Labradoodle types to cause allergies.

Labradoodles come in many different colors. A Labradoodle's coat might be black, yellow, or brown. Other Labradoodle coat colors include cream, red, silver, or white. A Labradoodle's coat can also be more than one color.

Some Labradoodles have coats with patches of different colors.

CHAPTER FOUR

CARING FOR YOUR LABRADOODLE

Before deciding to get a Labradoodle, your family should think about what a Labradoodle will need. All dogs should be **groomed**. Grooming includes brushing and combing your dog's coat. Brushing cleans the dog's coat. Combing keeps it free of tangles.

Some Labradoodles have shorter coats that do not tangle. Owners can groom these types of Labradoodles at home. Other Labradoodles have longer fleece or wool coats. Special equipment is needed to groom these types of coats. People who own these types of Labradoodles should take their dogs to a professional groomer about once every four to six weeks.

 groom – to care for a dog's coat

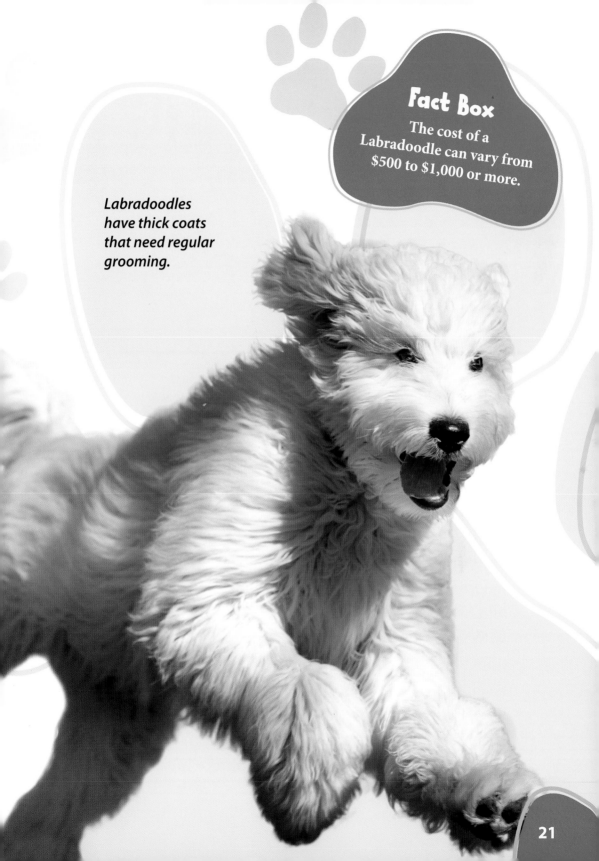

Labradoodles have thick coats that need regular grooming.

DIET AND EXERCISE

Like all dogs, Labradoodles need exercise and a healthful diet. Most Labradoodles need 30 to 60 minutes of exercise each day. Your veterinarian can recommend the best type of food for your dog. Most Labradoodles eat one to two and a half cups of food per day. The amount varies depending on your dog's size. You should split the food into two meals each day.

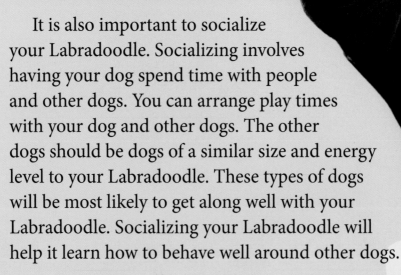

Fact Box

Some Labradoodles are good at dock diving. Dock diving is a type of competition in which a person throws an object from a dock into water. The dog that jumps the farthest wins!

It is also important to socialize your Labradoodle. Socializing involves having your dog spend time with people and other dogs. You can arrange play times with your dog and other dogs. The other dogs should be dogs of a similar size and energy level to your Labradoodle. These types of dogs will be most likely to get along well with your Labradoodle. Socializing your Labradoodle will help it learn how to behave well around other dogs.

Labradoodles love to run and play.

When Labradoodles swim, moisture can become trapped in their ears and cause infection.

LABRADOODLE HEALTH

Both poodles and Labrador retrievers tend to develop hip dysplasia. Labradoodles could **inherit** this condition. In hip dysplasia, the upper leg bone does not fit snugly into the hip joint. Labradoodles might also develop elbow dysplasia. This condition usually occurs when a dog's elbow bones do not grow properly. It causes swelling and joint pain in a dog's elbow. Dysplasia is painful. Dogs who have dysplasia will often develop a limp.

Another health problem that Labradoodles may develop is progressive retinal atrophy (PRA). The retina is a part of the eye. It receives images and sends signals to the brain so the brain can identify images. PRA damages the retina over time. A dog with PRA will lose part or all of its vision.

Labradoodles can get ear **infections**. Ear infections can happen when moisture gets inside a dog's ears. Then germs can get into the ear. Ear infections cause ear pain and difficulty hearing. A Labradoodle's floppy ears easily trap moisture, especially when it swims. After a swim, dry your dog's ears carefully. Check your dog's ears at least once a week for signs of infection, such as redness or a bad smell.

inherit – to get a trait from a parent or ancestor

infection – a condition that occurs when germs such as bacteria and viruses get inside the body of a person or animal

Veterinarians can usually treat these health issues with medicine or surgery. Sometimes a special diet and exercise help these problems get better. You should take your Labradoodle to the veterinarian at least once a year for a checkup. Your veterinarian will also give your Labradoodle regular **vaccination** shots. These shots help protect your Labradoodle against diseases.

 vaccination – a shot of a medicine that prevents a person or animal from getting a disease

Your family should also talk to your veterinarian about having your Labradoodle neutered or spayed. Neutering involves removing a part of a male animal's body that helps it make babies. Spaying is a similar process, but it is done for a female animal. These surgeries can keep your dog from having puppies. Dogs that aren't spayed or neutered can have many puppies. It can be hard for one family to take care of or find a home for many puppies.

Regular visits to the veterinarian can help keep your Labradoodle healthy.

CHOOSING A LABRADOODLE

If your family is ready to get a Labradoodle, searching for a licensed breeder is a good place to start. Your family should ask the breeder whether the dog has been to a veterinarian and received all of the shots it needs. The breeder should give you the veterinarian's records. The breeder should also give you information about the Labradoodle's family history. This will help you find out if any health conditions run in the dog's family. Your family could also try finding a Labradoodle at a rescue agency or dog shelter. People at the agency or shelter may have information about the dog's background.

Having a pet is a big responsibility. But it is also a lot of fun. If you like to get outside and move, the Labradoodle may be the perfect dog for you and your family.

Labradoodles are beloved members of many families.

GLOSSARY

breed (BREED)—a type of dog that has specific traits

breeder (BREED-ur)—someone who brings dogs together so they can breed, or reproduce

groom (GROOM)—to care for a dog's coat

guide dog (GIDE DAWG)—a dog that helps people with vision problems move around safely

infection (in-FEK-shuhn)—a condition that occurs when germs such as bacteria and viruses get inside the body of a person or animal

inherit (in-HAIR-it)—to get a trait from a parent or ancestor

litter (LIH-tur)—a group of puppies born from the same mother

purebred (PYOOR-bred)—a dog that is the same breed as its parents

quarantine (KWOR-uhn-teen)—a place where an animal is kept alone until proven healthy so it doesn't spread disease

texture (TEKS-chur)—the feel of something, such as a dog's fur

vaccination (VAK-suh-nay-shuhn)—a shot of a medicine that prevents a person or animal from getting a disease

READ MORE

Gagne, Tammy. *Bulldogs, Poodles, Dalmatians, and Other Non-Sporting Dogs.* Dog Encyclopedias. North Mankato, Minn.: Capstone Press, 2017.

Gagne, Tammy. *Spaniels, Retrievers, and Other Sporting Dogs.* Dog Encyclopedias. North Mankato, Minn.: Capstone Press, 2017.

Jacobs, Pat. *Dog Pals.* Pet Pals. New York: Crabtree Publishing, 2018.

Roberts, Walter, Jr. *Therapy Dogs.* Dogs on the Job. North Mankato, Minn.: Capstone Press, 2014.

INTERNET SITES

Use FactHound to find Internet sites related to this book.

Visit www.facthound.com

Just type in 9781543555196 and go.

 **Super-cool stuff!** Check out projects, games and lots more at **www.capstonekids.com**

INDEX